America at Bat

Americ

Baseball Stuff & Stories

by Paul Rosenthal and the
National Baseball Hall of Fame
and Museum

NATIONAL GEOGRAPHIC
Washington, D.C.

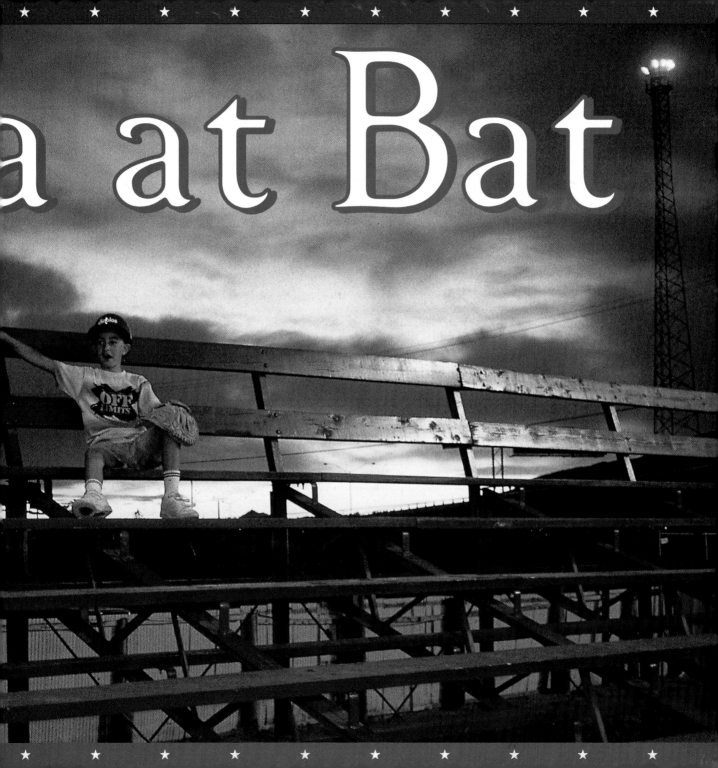

1869

The Cincinnati Red Stockings is the first team to describe itself as professional.

1876

Eight teams join to form the National League.

1880s

Baseball cards appear, promoting products—and players.

1900s

Harry M. Stevens begins selling hot dogs at New York's Polo Grounds. Fans cheer (and chew).

1901

The American League joins the fray as the country's second major league.

1909

Philadelphia welcomes Shibe Park, the first concrete-and-steel baseball stadium.

Published by the National Geographic Society.
All rights reserved. Reproduction of the whole or any part of the contents
without written permission from the National Geographic Society is strictly prohibited.

Book design by Bea Jackson and Dan Sherman.
Display and body text of the book are set in National Oldstyle.
Sidebars and captions are set in Century Gothic.
Illustrated cover and interior typography by Frank Frisari.

Library of Congress Cataloging-in-Publication Data

Rosenthal, Paul.
America at bat : baseball stuff and stories / by Paul Rosenthal.
p. cm.
Book to accompany the Baseball Hall of Fame's
Baseball as America traveling exhibit.
Summary: Examines how the game of baseball has evolved over the years
and become woven into American culture and traditions,
highlights baseball heroes, and presents trivia questions.
ISBN 0-7922-6490-8
1. Baseball—United States—History—Juvenile literature.
[1. Baseball—History.] I. National Baseball Hall of Fame and Museum.
II. Title.
GV867.5 .R67 2002
796.357'0973—dc21
2002000144

Printed in Spain

1939

The National Baseball Hall of Fame and Museum officially opens in Cooperstown, New York.

1943

The All-American Girls Professional Baseball League plays its first game.

1947

Jackie Robinson—modern-day baseball's first African-American major league player—joins the Brooklyn Dodgers lineup.

1951

The final game of the Dodgers-Giants playoff is the first baseball contest televised nationwide.

1956

Yankee Don Larsen pitches a perfect game against the Dodgers in Game Five of the World Series.

1961

Major League Baseball expands for the first time, adding two new teams.

1917

The St. Louis Cardinals form the first major league knothole gang, a kids' fan club.

1920

The Negro National League takes the field as the first of the modern Negro leagues.

1921

The first radio broadcast of a major league game introduces a new way to enjoy baseball.

1927

Babe Ruth becomes the first player to hit 60 home runs in a single season.

1933

Baseball's best gather in Chicago for the first modern All-Star Game.

1935

The lights go on for the first major league night game, at Cincinnati's Crosley Field.

1966

The Houston Astrodome is the first stadium to install AstroTurf, or artificial grass.

1973

The American League's new designated hitter rule lets a substitute player bat in place of the pitcher.

1974

San Diego's Chicken struts onto the field. He's the first of baseball's furry (or feathered) mascots.

1980

Former Cub Randy Hundley launches the first baseball "fantasy camp," where big dreamers play big-leaguers.

1998

Cal Ripken plays his 2,632nd consecutive game, the last in a streak that began in 1982.

2001

Seattle's Ichiro Suzuki becomes the major league's first position player from Japan.

As a child, I played baseball with an old broomstick and some rolled-up rags. Nothing compared to smacking that makeshift ball, my friends chasing it, and me running full speed for home plate. Baseball taught me at an early age that achievement comes from resourcefulness, hard work, and making the most of each opportunity.

That's why the game is our National Pastime. On the field, everyone has an equal chance to succeed. Everyone gets the same number of strikes, the same number of balls, and the same shot at making the catch or hitting the home run. Your skin color or how much money you have doesn't matter. When you play baseball, you get a turn at bat just like the next kid.

America at Bat captures the thrill of the home run, the cheers of the crowd, and the excitement of each new record. I set a few of those records in my career. But I'm guessing one day maybe some kid who reads this book—black, white, Asian, or Latino—will hit more home runs than me. Whoever it is, I will be pulling for him…or her.

Hank Aaron

HENRY "HANK" AARON
CHAIRMAN, CHASING THE DREAM FOUNDATION

Hall of Famer Hank Aaron smashed a record 755 homers. Today, Aaron's Chasing the Dream Foundation offers financial aid to help kids with special talents achieve *their* goals.

In 1909, kids improvise a game of baseball amid the drying laundry in a city alley.

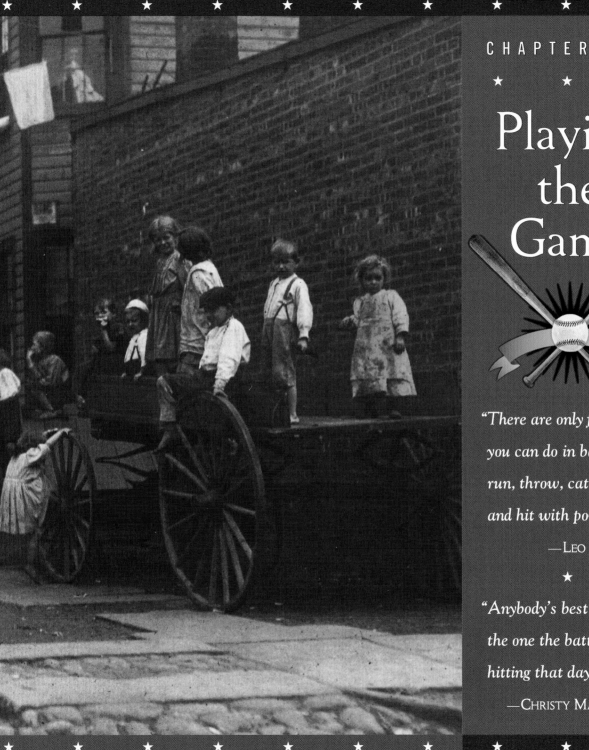

CHAPTER ONE

Playing the Game

"There are only five things you can do in baseball— run, throw, catch, hit, and hit with power."

—LEO DUROCHER

★

"Anybody's best pitch is the one the batters ain't hitting that day."

—CHRISTY MATHEWSON

When you think of baseball, what comes to mind? Crowds and Cracker Jack? Star players? Hot dogs? All are part of the game. All make fans feel good (unless you eat too many hot dogs). But baseball is *really* about a bat, a ball, and bases. It's about playing the game.

TOOLS OF THE TEAM

What do you need to play baseball? First, you need a baseball. In the major leagues, regulation balls are crafted of yarn wrapped around rubber and cork, covered with strips of stitched white cowhide (which is enough to make any cow hide). Some amateur and kids' leagues use softer, safer balls.

Next, you'll need a bat. Traditionally, bats are wooden, but there are aluminum bats, too. These usually send the ball farther and faster because metal doesn't absorb as much of the energy as the softer wood.

Americans young and old play baseball. *Opposite:* Jackie Robinson's Dodgers jersey (circa 1956), glove (circa 1947), and cap (circa 1955). *Right:* Gloria Cordes Elliott's tunic, from Michigan's Kalamazoo Lassies, 1954. *Top:* Glove used by Orioles third baseman Brooks Robinson in the 1970 World Series.

DIGGING UP DIAMONDS With its broad, grassy fields and leisurely pace, you might expect baseball to be a country or small-town game—which it is. But baseball's a city game, too. The earliest recorded match, in fact, was in New York City in 1823. The first officially professional team formed in Cincinnati in 1869. Most major league stadiums are in big cities. Of course, colleges, suburban communities, and small towns host teams as well.

So, country or city? Stadium or sandlot? Where's the best place to play baseball? Wherever you happen to be.

Players today generally wear a fielding glove. They didn't always. Doug Allison of the 1869 Cincinnati Red Stockings was the first known glove-wearer. His gloves (he wore two!) were fingerless, intended to prevent sore hands. Webbed gloves came later.

To improve comfort, safety, and their team's odds of winning, players have invented all sorts of other equipment, from batting helmets to shin guards. In the 1970s, someone devised a catcher's mitt with orange reflectors—great for night games. It didn't catch on.

FOLLOWING THE RULES

As America's first professional team sport, baseball quickly developed "official" organizations. Leagues and, later, commissioners established basic rules, such as each team having nine players on the field. (America's Supreme Court also establishes rules and has nine people—but they all stay on the bench.)

Some rules were set early on. Players *always* hit balls and ran bases. Other rules evolved gradually. Not until the 1880s did batters get a free ticket to first base if whacked by a pitch.

Above, left to right: Spalding's Official Base Ball Guide, 1890; DeWitt's Base Ball Umpire's Guide, 1875; and The Reach Art of Curve Pitching, an 1888 instruction book.

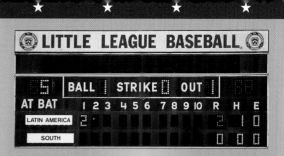

KID STUFF Professional players grab headlines, so it's easy to forget that baseball is a game. And when it comes to games, kids rule!

Little League Baseball has thrived since Carl Stotz founded the organization in 1939. Today, Little League spans 100 countries (making its championship truly a *World Series*). Kids step up to the plate in dozens of other groups, too, from the American Amateur Baseball Congress to the Babe Ruth League and Police Athletic leagues.

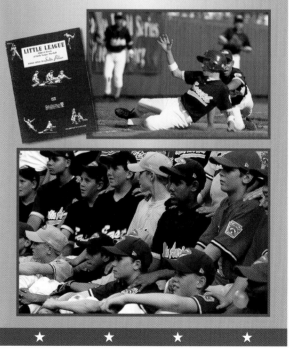

MATTERS OF STYLE

Batting and pitching—those are the most essential player skills (though being able to sign your name on a round ball takes skill, too). Those two simple activities, however, embrace tremendous variations in style and technique.

Some batters, such as Mark McGwire or Babe Ruth, are sluggers, known for power. Others, like Ty Cobb and Tony Gwynn, emphasize a more precise "scientific" approach. Pitchers also vary, from Cy Young and Randy Johnson's furious fastballs to the amazing accuracy of Satchel Paige and Greg Maddux.

Every team member has to master the basic skills of throwing and hitting, plus catching and fielding. Most baseball players, however, have some particular area of strength. *Above, right:* Batting champ Maurice "Mo" Vaughn, 1995's American League MVP, swings for the Anaheim Angels in 2000. *Below, left:* A 1995 stop-action sequence of Dodger Hideki Nomo captures the ball-throwing ballet of an overhand pitch. *Below, right:* Hall of Famer Robin Yount, playing for the Milwaukee Brewers, slides into base during a 1990 match against Kansas City.

1. They say that "a stitch in time saves nine"—but it takes more stitches to satisfy a baseball team of nine. Regulation balls use
A) 57 stitches.
B) 108 stitches.
C) 131 stitches.
D) Super Glue.

2. What did Yankee Ron Blomberg do in 1973?
A) He started the fad of wearing a baseball cap backward.
B) He stole a record 97 bases (then gave them back).
C) He became the first designated hitter in the majors.
D) He scored the first touchdown ever at a World Series.

RON BLOMBERG

Find the answers on page 48.

Quiz

★ ★ ★ ★ ★

SLIDING INTO HOME PLATE, 2001

3. What did 30 boys do in Williamsport, Pennsylvania, in 1939?
A) Not much. It was a dull year.
B) They formed the first three Little League teams.
C) They created baseball's first official fan club.
D) They invented T-ball.

4. What made Houston's Astrodome special when it opened in 1965?
A) It was the biggest stadium ever built.

B) Its players were astronauts from Houston's Johnson Space Center.
C) It was baseball's first covered stadium.
D) It was the first new stadium built after World War II.

5. The first night game in major league history was played
A) at Brooklyn's Ebbets Field in 1929.
B) at Cincinnati's Crosley Field in 1935.
C) at Chicago's Wrigley Field in 1947.
D) at night.

NIGHT BASE BALL
BY ELECTRIC FLOOD LIGHTS
KANSAS CITY MONARCHS
vs CONCORDIA
Tuesday, Sept. 16
Fairground, Concordia   8 P. M.

ASSORTED NIGHT GAME MEMORABILIA

CHAPTER TWO

Cheering the Game

"A hot dog at the ball-park is better than steak at the Ritz."

—HUMPHREY BOGART

★

"Then from 5,000 throats and more there rose a lusty yell."

—from *Casey at the Bat*, ERNEST L. THAYER

Kids whoop for a winner at a 1999 Texas Rangers vs. Kansas City Royals Hall of Fame exhibition game in Cooperstown, New York.

Players. Managers. Scouts. Team owners. Umpires. Broadcasters. Hot dog vendors. Who's missing from this baseball lineup?

You are. Fans don't just watch games, they're part of them. Cheering inspires players. Fans attending games support stadiums (and stadiums support fan fannies).

THE STUFF OF DREAMS

Did you hear that Randy Johnson was traded for Roger Clemens? Maybe not...because it was two kids in Montana who made the trade. They swapped cards.

Thanks to baseball cards, first made as advertisements in the 1860s and widespread as product inserts since the 1880s, *everyone* can get into the act. Similarly, games, souvenirs, knickknacks,

Who needs a diamond to play baseball? *Opposite:* Cards let collectors "own" a team. *Left, clockwise from top:* Parlor Base Ball, an 1878 board game; Lawson's Patent Base Ball Playing Cards, 1884; and Fan Craze, 1904. *Right, left to right:* Pennants circa 1955, 1910, and 1968. *Top:* Hand-painted baseball by George Sosnak (1971) celebrates the Tigers' new training facility in Florida.

FROM THE STADIUM TO A STORE NEAR YOU Next time you're at a mall or a schoolyard, or on a crowded street, count the baseball caps. You'll probably run out of patience long before you run out of caps. Our national game has become our national hat! Baseball's role in our daily lives—and the products we buy—doesn't end with clothing, however.

Candy bars, fishing line, chewing gum—almost every product you can imagine has had some link to baseball. And quite a few products you wouldn't imagine, too. Ever hear of Babe Ruth Underwear? Your great-grandparents probably did. (With such a famous baseball player selling underwear, why are men's shorts known as boxers and jockeys?)

Baseball-related goodies have filled store shelves since the 19th century. Many are the work of advertisers hoping that the game's popularity will help to sell their stuff. Fans buy baseball-themed products—including Babe Ruth Underwear—because it gives them a way to take a bit of the game home. It's certainly simpler to keep a team cap in your closet than the team itself. (And you don't have to feed a hat.)

Today, you're particularly likely to come face-to-face with baseball players across the breakfast table, staring out at you from a cereal box. (From a picture on the box, that is, not from the box itself. You'd have a hard time squishing Roger Clemens or Nolan Ryan into a carton of cereal flakes. And you probably wouldn't want to eat the flakes afterward.) Putting sports figures on cereal packages began in 1935 when Wheaties featured Olympic athletes on its "Breakfast of Champions." Soon after, Wheaties began using baseball players, printing card-size images (for fans to cut out) of Mickey Cochrane, Lou Gehrig, and many others.

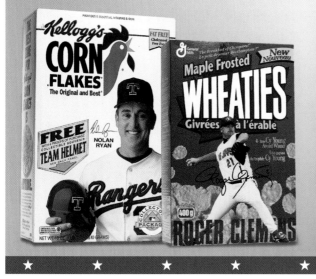

and all sorts of collectibles turn baseball fans into baseball "owners." Your favorite teams and players become yours, to enjoy, keep, take home—or trade.

COME ONE, COME ALL

What do umbrellas have to do with baseball? Not much. They're too fluffy to use as bats, and an ump would never let you catch a ball in one (though it would be a cool trick). Yet, on Umbrella Day, stadiums look like a rainy day in London.

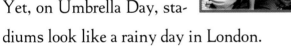

Special events are an old baseball tradition, from Ladies Day, a promotion to attract more women, to Cap Day and Old Timers' Day. If it will draw a crowd, some team somewhere has probably tried it.

In the 1950s, Browns owner Bill Veeck, whose "You Be the Manager Night" once let fans in the stands vote on strategy, was master of the outlandish stunt.

Top: Crowds clamor for autographs at Arlington Stadium in Texas, 1994. *Left:* Kansas City's Kaufman Stadium blossoms with umbrellas, June 2000; a youngster meets Texas Ranger Rafael Palmeiro at Camden Yards, 2000. *Right:* A fan grabs for a souvenir at Chicago's Comiskey Park, 1997.

7TH INNING STRETCH

ALL TOGETHER NOW

Ballpark rituals unite and involve fans. We don't just watch, we join in. Fans aren't invited to bat, of course. But they do catch. In 1998, when Sammy Sosa became the second player to hit 62 homers in one season, Brendan Cunningham made news by retrieving Sosa's ball. That sort of thing is common in baseball—and rare everywhere else. Ever hear of a basketball fan retrieving Shaquille O'Neal's ball?

There are lots of ballpark rituals, from eating hot dogs to standing for the seventh inning stretch. Harry Caray, baseball broadcaster from 1944 to 1997, led sing-alongs of "Take Me Out to the Ball Game" during seventh inning stretches at Wrigley Field. Today, the tradition has spread almost everywhere.

DESIGNATED CRITTERS

What do a chicken, a parrot, and a seal have to do with baseball? A lot. They, and other mascots, lead us in cheering our heroes. They also entertain us, which is important too. Folks in the stands are watching a show.

From the major leagues' famed Phillie Phanatic to the Pioneer League's somewhat less famous Spokane-asaurus, mascots encourage fans… whose rooting encourages players.

At a 2001 T-ball game on the White House lawn, The Famous Chicken greets a not-yet-famous player.

Find the answers on page 48.

Quiz

1. When Jack Norworth and Albert von Tilzer wrote "Take Me Out to the Ball Game" in 1908
   A) they'd never written a song before.
   B) they'd never been to a major league ballgame.
   C) they'd never met each other.
   D) they were players in different leagues.

CLOCKWISE FROM TOP LEFT: DEREK JETER, 1995; HONUS WAGNER, 1909; MICHAEL JORDAN, 1991, AND BABE RUTH, 1948

2. The most valuable baseball card is currently worth about $1.2 million. Who's on it, and what year was it made?
   A) Derek Jeter (1995)
   B) Babe Ruth (1948)
   C) Honus Wagner (1909)
   D) Michael Jordan (1991)

3. How (and when) did fans gain the right to keep foul balls hit into the stands?
   A) From a 1921 court case
   B) After Harry Truman's 1950 presidential catch
   C) Thanks to Congress's 1894 "Finders, Keepers" law
   D) In a 1943 ruling by Commissioner Landis

4. Each season, on average, fans at every major league stadium
   A) do the hokey-pokey at least once.
   B) buy 27,000 hot dogs.
   C) sing "Take Me Out to the Ball Game" ⅛ tone flat.
   D) eat 13,500 gallons of mustard.

À LA CART ON OPENING DAY, CINCINNATI, OHIO

5. Hilda Chester loved the Brooklyn Dodgers. How did she show it?
   A) She married Pee Wee Reese.
   B) She rang a cow bell at home games from the 1930s to 1957.
   C) She knitted sweaters for every Dodger each season.
   D) She sang "Brooklyn Rag" before most home games from 1944 to 1952.

GIVE THAT FAN A CONTRACT!

The United States Olympic Baseball Team celebrates its gold medal at the 2000 Summer Olympics in Sydney, Australia.

CHAPTER THREE

Heroes of the Game

"I think there are some players who are born to play ball."

—JOE DiMAGGIO

★

"I want to be remembered as a ball player who gave all he had to give."

—ROBERTO CLEMENTE

W hy do we look up to certain people? Well, yes…we look up to some because they're taller. Why else? What makes a hero a hero?

FIGHTER FOR FAIRNESS

Imagine that you're choosing players for a team. There's one kid who's great at fielding *and* batting, is dying to play—and is African American. Would you choose him?

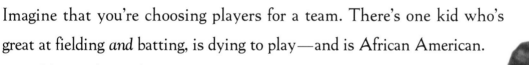

Opposite: The 1935 Pittsburgh Crawfords team included future Hall of Famers Josh Gibson, Oscar Charleston, and Satchel Paige. *Above:* Jackie Robinson steals home in 1952. *Top:* Pittsburgh Crawfords jersey, 1938, and artifacts from the Negro leagues and baseball's segregated era.

Who wouldn't?

Well, for many years, Major League Baseball wouldn't. Discrimination kept African Americans and many Latinos off "white" teams—until Jackie Robinson and the majors changed that in 1947.

Robinson had already proven himself a star at UCLA in the 1930s, and later drew crowds for the Negro National League's Kansas City Monarchs. He had proven

himself a civil rights fighter, too. During World War II, Robinson was court-martialed for refusing to sit in the back of a military bus. "There is not an American in this country free until every one of us is free," he once observed.

Not everyone was happy when Dodgers general manager Branch Rickey hired a black player. There were catcalls and hate mail. Nevertheless, Robinson played with courage, dignity, and skill. In ten years on the team, he was a six-time All-Star and hit .311, becoming a baseball hero *and* an American hero.

NOT ALL HEROES ARE FAMOUS "Keep your eye on the ball," players are told. It's good advice. But what if you're blind? With a beeping Pioneer Audio Ball, you don't have to see to swing. You just need the courage to try.

That spirit thrives in Little League's Challenger Division for mentally and physically disabled children. These kids remind us that heroism is *not* about how well you play or how much you earn. It's about who you are.

FAME!

Remember in *The Wizard of Oz* when the Cowardly Lion gets a medal? It didn't give the Lion courage, but it *seemed* to. That reflects the importance of celebrating heroes *officially*—which is what the National Baseball Hall of Fame and Museum does.

Top: Kirby Puckett signs autographs at the Hall of Fame, 2001. *Above, left to right:* Joe DiMaggio's 1951 jersey; tickets to the Lou Gehrig Memorial Game in 1941; Ty Cobb's Hall of Fame plaque; DiMaggio at bat.

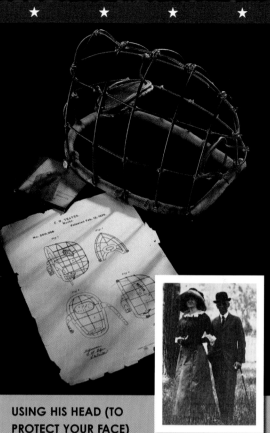

USING HIS HEAD (TO PROTECT YOUR FACE)

Most baseball heroes win cheers from fans. Fred Thayer won cheers from fellow players.

Thayer, captain of the Harvard Base Ball Club from 1876 to 1878, noticed that catchers didn't play their best when they were nervous about getting knocked on the noggin by a fastball. He also noticed that fencers wore masks to protect their faces.

Putting the two ideas together, Thayer sketched plans for baseball's first catcher's mask. It quickly caught on, giving players newfound confidence that often translated into the winning edge.

One story tells of Babe Ruth visiting a sick 11-year-old in the hospital, promising the boy he would hit a World Series homer—then keeping his promise a few days later.

Another story recounts how Ruth, at Wrigley Field in Chicago, let two strikes pass in the 1932 World Series. He then pointed to the center field fence and hit the ball out of the park in just that spot.

A giant on the diamond and a media favorite, the colorful Babe became a sports legend and an American superstar. Six decades after the Bambino's retirement, his star still shines.

Movies and radio appeared about the same time as Ruth, and both helped to make him a superstar. *Above:* George Herman "Babe" Ruth hits the ball. *Right:* A poster announces Ruth's 1924 appearance in Los Angeles; the bat that Ruth used to hit his record-breaking 60th season homer in 1927.

JACKIE ROBINSON ENTERS THE DODGERS CLUB HOUSE FOR THE FIRST TIME, 1947.

DODGERS
CLUB HOUSE

KEEP OUT

Find the answers on page 48.

Quiz

★ ★ ★ ★ ★

JOE NUXHALL

1. Jackie Robinson made history in 1947 as the first African American in the majors. Who made history in 1947 as baseball's first-ever Rookie of the Year?
A) Sammy Sosa
B) Joe DiMaggio
C) Mickey Mantle
D) Jackie Robinson

2. When Babe Ruth joined the majors, and Stan Musial the minors, they were recognized as talented
A) pitchers.
B) batters.
C) catchers.
D) hot dog vendors.

STAN MUSIAL

3. When did the All-American Girls Professional Baseball League begin—and why then?
A) 1776—because Martha Washington threw a wicked curve
B) 1929—to cheer up folks at the start of the Great Depression
C) 1943—while many male players fought in WWII
D) 1977—sparked by the women's rights movement

4. Why was 15-year-old Joe Nuxhall a hero to many kids in 1944?
A) He pitched for the Cincinnati Reds.
B) He was Little League's MVP.
C) He really aced his math test.
D) He sold his Babe Ruth card for $1 million.

5. What made Masanori Murakami so noteworthy in 1964?
A) He toured with The Beatles, playing first bass.
B) Both his names start with M and end with I.
C) He introduced baseball to Japan.
D) He was the first Japanese pitcher in the major leagues.

MASANORI MURAKAMI

ONE OF THE GRAND RAPIDS CHICKS GLIDES HOME.

CHAPTER FOUR

America's Game

"*I am never more at home in America than at a baseball game.*"

—ROBERT FROST

★

"*Whoever wants to know the heart and mind of America had better learn baseball.*"

—JACQUES BARZUN

"The American National Game of Base Ball," an 1866 Currier & Ives print, reflects the sport's early identification as the National Pastime.

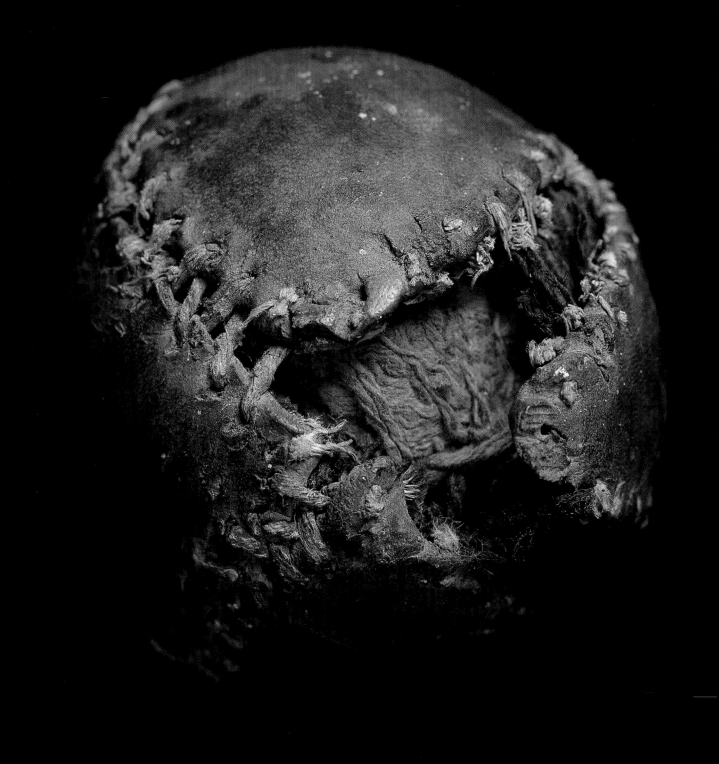

Americans love all sorts of sports, from football to Ping-Pong. But only baseball has earned the title of National Pastime. Only baseball is thoroughly woven into American culture, traditions, and history.

Think about it. You've probably sung "Take Me Out to the Ball Game" and read "Casey at the Bat." How many football songs or Ping-Pong poems do you know?

THE STAR-SPANGLED SPORT

Baseball is as American as apple pie (and vanilla ice cream goes great with both). The game evolved in the early 1800s, a time when the United States was beginning to define itself and develop new traditions. The nation and the game grew up together. And, like kids who grow up together, each influenced the other. Baseball would not be baseball without

Opposite: An old, homemade ball found near Cooperstown in 1934 seemed to offer proof of baseball's birth there. Called the "Doubleday Ball," it became part of the myth. *Left:* A 1917 World Series program shows President Wilson tossing 1916's "first pitch." *Top:* A miniature of Douglas Tilden's sculpture "The Baseball Player," 1888–1889, now in San Francisco's Golden Gate Park.

America—and America would not be America without baseball.

But was America's game truly an American creation?

People hoped so. In the early 1900s, a commission headed by National League president A. G. Mills gathered evidence. In 1907, the Mills Commission declared "officially" that General Abner Doubleday, a Civil War hero, had invented baseball in Cooperstown, New York, in 1839. America cheered. Not only was baseball invented here, it was invented by a hero!

Today, new research shows that baseball is older,

TAKING AMERICA ABROAD New York, St. Louis, Chicago, the Great Pyramid at Giza in Egypt—which of these *didn't* host American baseball teams in the 1880s?

If you guessed the Great Pyramid, you're wrong. Americans played in *all* these spots. (Don't you hate trick questions!) Egypt was a stop on the 1888–1889 world tour.

This wasn't baseball's first time as an ambassador of our culture and values. And it certainly wasn't its last. Players have represented America everywhere, from China in 1913 to Cuba in 1999.

Who invented America's game? *Right*: A 1905 essay by A. G. Spalding, baseball pioneer and sporting goods manufacturer, challenges Henry Chadwick's suggestion that the game originated in Britain.

that it evolved gradually, and that General Doubleday probably played no role. But when it comes to national myths, accuracy is often less important than symbolism. The beloved Doubleday tale lives on.

And why shouldn't it? After all, that yarn about George Washington chopping down a cherry tree isn't true, yet we still tell it because the story symbolizes George's honesty, just as the Doubleday and Cooperstown myths have come to symbolize the all-American roots of America's national game.

THE NATIONAL GAME

You won't find William Howard Taft on any baseball card. He's not in the Hall of Fame. Still, Taft *did* make baseball history in 1910. Guess why.

Politicians as far back as Abe Lincoln have enjoyed a link to baseball's all-American reputation. *Right*: President Taft tosses the season's first ball in Washington D.C., circa 1911.

THE SPIRIT OF AMERICA Americans often use baseball to express patriotism and pride. After the September 11, 2001, terrorist attacks, stadiums became "town squares" where citizens shared feelings—as in a September 17, 2001, pre-game memorial in Philadelphia.

Baseball in turn uses patriotic symbols to promote and define itself. For example, on the July 1908 cover of *The Baseball Magazine,* Uncle Sam winds up to pitch the sport—and also helps illustrate the game's special place as an American institution.

Our National Game   Our National Holiday
THE
BASEBALL
MAGAZINE
JULY
1908

Shall We
Have
Sunday
Baseball?

PRICE
15 CENTS
$1.50
A YEAR

Give up? Taft began the tradition of American Presidents throwing the first pitch on Opening Day. Nearly every President since has followed him as "pitcher in chief." Appearing in the grandstands, tossing a ball, maybe munching a hot dog, and of course singing the national anthem link them to a powerful American symbol. For baseball, having leaders participate strengthens its position as our National Pastime.

Over the decades, all manner of products, movies, and songs have used baseball themes to express patriotism or show their American-ness. Baseball, meanwhile, encourages this close relationship between the American nation and America's game by flying flags, playing the national anthem, and promoting foreign tours by U.S. teams.

1. "The Star-Spangled Banner" made its major league debut at the 1918 World Series. Why?
A) It was Babe Ruth's favorite song.
B) The organist was sick of "Take Me Out to the Ball Game."
C) It demonstrated patriotism during World War I.
D) "God Bless America" hadn't been written yet.

THE FLAG THAT INSPIRED FRANCIS SCOTT KEY TO WRITE *THE STAR-SPANGLED BANNER* IN 1814

2. Why is the National Baseball Hall of Fame in the village of Cooperstown, New York?
A) Why not?
B) Major League Baseball's first Commissioner lived in Cooperstown.

C) Abner Doubleday was mayor of Cooperstown.
D) Legend claimed that baseball was invented there.

3. Which famous American was a former radio announcer for America's game?
A) Ronald Reagan
B) George S. Patton
C) Elvis Presley
D) Bill Clinton

4. President William Howard Taft strengthened ties between the White House and baseball by
A) proclaiming April 14, 1910, "National Baseball Day."

B) throwing out the first pitch on Opening Day, 1910.
C) inviting the Yankees and White Sox to play on the White House lawn.
D) taking a weekend job as manager of the Washington Senators.

METS VS. CUBS, MARCH 29, 2001, AND THE METS MASCOT

5. The New York Mets and Chicago Cubs opened America's 2000 major league season in
A) New York.
B) Chicago.
C) Tokyo, Japan.
D) their pajamas.

THE NATIONAL BASEBALL HALL OF FAME AND MUSEUM, COOPERSTOWN, NEW YORK

Julie Croteau, pioneering female baseball player, cracked the starting lineup for St. Mary's College (Maryland) in 1989. Here, she plays in an NCAA game against Gallaudet University.

CHAPTER FIVE

Firsts in the Game

"Statistics are to baseball
what a flaky crust is to
Mom's apple pie."

—HARRY REASONER

★

"I hope someday my son
grows up to be a baseball
player and breaks the
record."

—MARK MCGWIRE

Fans chuckle at Abbott and Costello's baseball routine, "Who's on First"—but it's the question "Who *Was* First?" that *really* gets their attention. Being first to do something earns a place in the history books—including this one.

PLAY FOR PLAY

Ball clubs began as just that: clubs. Friends got together to get a bit of exercise and to chill. (They didn't call it "chilling," of course. If you invited folks in the 1830s to chill, they'd bring a sweater.) Baseball was a game, not a job.

As ballparks began charging admission in the 1860s, winning became more important—

particularly to investors. Owners began offering money to attract top players. In 1869, the Cincinnati Red Stockings began describing themselves as professional. They're considered baseball's first professional team.

Opposite: Houston's Astrodome, baseball's first indoor stadium, April 1965. *Left:* The 1869 Cincinnati Red Stockings. *Top:* The silver 2000 World Series trophy, designed by Tiffany & Co.

RICKEY HENDERSON

FRANK ROBINSON

THE FIRST NIGHT GAME, CINCINNATI VS. PHILADELPHIA

BARRY BONDS WITH HIS SON NIKOLAI

FIRST STOLEN BASE In the 1860s, the Philadelphia Keystones' Ned Cuthbert ran from first to second before the ball was hit. The crowd laughed. When Cuthbert pointed out that there was no rule against it, he had the last laugh—and the first recorded stolen base. Rickey Henderson is first in stolen bases, the all-time leader, now at 1,395.

FIRST SWITCH-HIT HOMERS In 1916, Philadelphia's Wally Schang was the first to smash switch-hit homers (from both the right and left sides of the plate) in the same game.

WALLY SCHANG

FIRST AFRICAN-AMERICAN MANAGER Hired by the Cleveland Indians in 1975, Frank Robinson became the first African-American manager in the majors — nearly 30 years after Jackie Robinson "broke the color line."

LOU GEHRIG, YANKEE STADIUM, JULY 4, 1939

FIRST NUMBER RETIRED Yankee star Lou Gehrig left baseball abruptly in 1939 after being stricken with amyotrophic lateral sclerosis (known as Lou Gehrig's disease). Gehrig was the first player honored by having his number retired.

FIRST FOUR-TIME MVP In 2001, Barry Bonds became the majors' first four-time MVP (and the first to hit his 500th and 550th homer in the same season).

FIRST NIGHT GAME President Franklin Roosevelt threw a switch at the White House on May 24, 1935, the signal to light Cincinnati's Crosley Field for the first major league night game. The Negro leagues and minor leagues tried lights earlier.

FIRST JERSEYS WITH NAMES To make it easier for TV viewers to recognize who's who, the White Sox and Cardinals put names on the backs of player uniforms in 1960. The idea caught on.

TED KLUSZEWSKI

FIRST TO BE BEST

Who won the first World Series? That depends on how you define "World Series."

In the 1880s, winners of various American matches often called themselves "World Champions." (It never occurred to anyone to include foreign teams in a "world" series.)

The World Series is more than just a match. It's an American institution. *Above:* The Boston Pilgrims and Pittsburgh Pirates meet at Boston's Huntington Avenue Grounds for the first modern World Series, 1903.

From 1892 to 1900, the National League was the only league. Nevertheless, its top teams competed in four "World's Championship Series" during that time.

The first modern World Series, in 1903, pitted the Boston Pilgrims (of the newly formed American League) against the Pittsburgh Pirates (National League). Boston won that best of nine series, 5–3. The next year, there was no World Series—because the New York Giants refused to go to Boston (the two teams weren't very chummy). The Series resumed in 1905 and continues today.

★ ★ ★ ★ ★ ★ ★ ★

TRYING TO BE FIRST Carolyn King wanted to play ball. So, like thousands of 12-year-olds, she joined Little League, playing for the Ypsilanti (Michigan) Orioles in 1973—until she was sent away because she was a girl. Carolyn sued for sex discrimination, as had others. She lost, but her spunk inspired still more lawsuits. The next year, Little League changed its rules and opened its teams to girls.

★ ★ ★ ★ ★ ★ ★ ★

THE GREAT RACE

Who's first among batters? The title keeps changing. In 1919, Babe Ruth slammed into the record books as first to hit 29 homers in one season. Ruth's record fell three times—to Babe Ruth. In 1927, Ruth hit 60, a total that even he couldn't top.

No one could until 1961, when Roger Maris and Mickey Mantle battled to beat the Babe. Maris succeeded, hitting 61.

The race heated up again in 1998 when Mark McGwire smashed 62 homers. Sammy Sosa did, too. Then Sosa slipped ahead. McGwire caught up. Sosa ended the season with 66 home runs. McGwire reached 70 by season's end.

With McGwire's record, you might think the race was over. Barry Bonds didn't. In 2001, he became first to hit 73 homers in one season.

Calling all batters! *Top*: Babe Ruth, 1924. *Bottom, left to right*: Roger Maris, 1961; Mickey Mantle brand blue jeans button; Barry Bonds; baseball cards for Sammy Sosa, Mark McGwire, and Barry Bonds.

1. What professional baseball "first" did Lee Richmond achieve in an 1880 Worcester vs. Cleveland game?

A) He was first to hit two home runs with a single swing.

B) He pitched the first "perfect game," with no batters reaching base.

C) He was first to use a bat made entirely of frozen fish sticks.

D) He hit the first tie-breaking home run in a World Series.

LOUISVILLE SLUGGER AND PETE BROWNING BASEBALL CARD, 1888

I find the answers on page 40.

2. How did Victoria Roche of Belgium make history in 1984?

A) She was the first woman to pitch for the New York Yankees.

B) She founded Europe's first professional baseball league.

C) She was the first girl to play in the Little League World Series.

D) She was the first female Olympic baseball player.

3. Pete Browning got three hits in three at-bats at an 1884 game. What made this a "first"?

A) He was the first to face a pitcher who threw over-hand.

B) It was the first time a pro-fessional player connected every time at bat.

C) He was the first to use a Louisville Slugger bat.

D) It was Browning's first game of baseball.

4. Hitting one homer is tough enough. Who was the first major leaguer to hit four in a single game?

A) Mickey Mantle (August 4, 1953)

B) Babe Ruth (June 26, 1921)

C) Honus Wagner (April 25, 1908)

D) Bobby Lowe (May 30, 1894)

BABE RUTH, CIRCA 1916   BILL WAMBSGANSS, 1923

5. What made Bill Wambsganss of the Cleveland Indians notable in 1920?

A) Even *he* couldn't spell his name.

B) He achieved the first and only unassisted triple play in World Series history.

C) He was the first and only pitcher to strike out Babe Ruth twice in one game.

D) Elected governor of Ohio, he was the first ex-player to succeed in politics.

Quiz
Answers

★ ★ ★ ★ ★

CHAPTER ONE
1B, 2C, 3B, 4C, 5B or D

CHAPTER TWO
1B, 2C, 3A, 4D, 5B

CHAPTER THREE
1D, 2A, 3C, 4A, 5D

CHAPTER FOUR
1C, 2D, 3A, 4B, 5C

CHAPTER FIVE
1B, 2C, 3C, 4D, 5B

★ ★ ★ ★ ★

ROCK CATS DUGOUT, NEW BRITAIN, CONNECTICUT

To the incomparable Albert Shmitzu, who knows everything about everything...except baseball. – PR

ACKNOWLEDGMENTS Special thanks go to the the following staff members of the National Baseball Hall of Fame and Museum: Jane Forbes Clark, Chairman; Dale Petroskey, President; Bill Haase, Senior Vice President; Jeff Idelson, Vice President, Communications and Education; Ted Spencer, Vice President and Chief Curator; Jim Gates, Library Director; Tim Wiles, Director of Research; Pat Kelly, Director of Photo Department; Milo Stewart, Photographer; W. C.Burdick, Senior Photo Researcher; John Odell, Curator of History and Research; Russ Wolinsky, Research Associate; Bill Francis, Senior Research Associate; Rachel Kepner, Research Associate, and Jeff Arnett, Director of Communications and Education.

PHOTO AND ILLUSTRATION CREDITS

NBHOFL-National Baseball Hall of Fame Library
NBHOFM-National Baseball Hall of Fame Museum

Cover, all artifacts by Milo Stewart Jr./NBHOF and Mark Thiessen, NGS with the exception of - World Series Baseball Tickets/Collection of Vincent P. Ryan

Chapter openers, baseball by Milo Stewart Jr./NBHOFL; crossed bats by Mark Thiessen, NGS

1 Milo Stewart Jr./NBHOFL; 2 William Albert Allard; 4 (top, l-r) NBHOFL; Mark Thiessen, NGS; Major League Baseball; Harry M. Stevens Family Foundation, Inc.; NBHOFL; 4 (bottom, l-r) NBHOFL; Northern Indiana Historical Society; NBHOFL; AP Photo; UPI/Corbis; Photo File; 5 (top, l-r) NBHOFL; NBHOFL; NBHOFL; NBHOFL; Earl D. Payne; 5 (bottom, l-r) NBHOFL; NBHOFL; TFC, Inc; Photo File; NBHOFM; Photo File; 6 Jonathan Newton/Atlanta Journal Constitution; 7 (top) Mark Thiessen, NGS; (bottom) NBHOFM; 8-9 Lewis W. Hine/George Eastman House; 10-11 (all) Mark Thiessen, NGS; 12 (l-r) Don Howard/NBHOFL; NBHOFL; Steve Green/Chicago Cubs; 13 (bottom left, l-r) Milo Stewart Jr./NBHOFL; Milo Stewart Jr./NBHOFM; Mark Thiessen, NGS; (top right, ctr, bottom) Major League Baseball Photos; (center left) Milo Stewart Jr./NBHOFM; 14 (top) Photo File; (bottom left) V. J.Lovero; (bottom right) Hank Koshollek/The Capital Times; 15 (left) NBHOFL; (center) Pete Souza; (right, both) Milo Stewart Jr./NBHOFM; 16-17 Philip Kamrass/Albany Times Union; 18 Mark Thiessen, NGS; 19 (top & lo left) Mark Thiessen, NGS; (bottom right) Milo Stewart Jr./NBHOFM; 20 (top) Milo Stewart Jr./NBHOFM; (bottom, both) Mark Thiessen, NGS; 21 (top) Mark Hertzberg/Racine Journal Times; (bottom left) Jim Barcus/Kansas City Star; (center) Courtesy Brady Bassford; (right) Jose M. Osorio/Chicago Tribune;

22 (top left) Major League Baseball Photo; (center) Milo Stewart Jr./NBHOFM; (bottom, both) Milo Stewart Jr./NBHOFM; (top right & center) David Barrett; (bottom) Linda J. Spillers; 23 (baseball cards starting clockwise from top left) Courtesy Lewis Bassford; Mark Thiessen, NGS; AP/Wide World Photos; NBHOFL; (top right) Andy Levin; (bottom) Paul Morse/Pasadena Star News; 24-25 USA Baseball/David Fanucchi; 26 NBHOFL; 27 (top) Mark Thiessen, NGS; (bottom) UPI/Corbis; 28 NBHOFL; 29 (clockwise starting top left) Milo Stewart Jr./NBHOFL; Mark Thiessen, NGS; NBHOFL; AP Photos; Milo Stewart Jr./NBHOFM; Milo Stewart Jr./NBHOFM; Milo Stewart Jr./NBHOFM; 30 (left) NBHOFL; (center) Milo Stewart Jr./NBHOFL; (right) Mark Thiessen, NGS; 31 (top left & bottom) NBHOFL; (center) Photo File; (top right) UPI/Corbis; (bottom) NBHOFL; 32-33 Currier & Ives/NBHOFL; 34 Mark Thiessen, NGS; 35 (top) Mark Thiessen, NGS; (bottom) Milo Stewart Jr./NBHOFL; 36 (top left) NBHOFL; (bottom) Mark Thiessen, NGS; (right) Milo Stewart Jr./NBHOFL; 37 (left) Mark Thiessen, NGS; (background) Mark Thiessen, NGS; (foreground) Brown Brothers; 38 (left) Milo Stewart Jr./ NBHOFL; (right) Reuters/Tim Shaffer; 39 (left) Photographic History Collection, National Museum of American History, Smithsonian Institution, neg. no. 83.7221; (center) NBHOFL; (right, both) Major League Baseball Photos; 40-41 Pete Souza; 42 NBHOFL; 43 (top) Tiffany & Co; (bottom) NBHOFL; 44 (top, l-r) Photo File; Mark Thiessen, NGS; Dino Vournas/Oakland Tribune; Earl D. Payne; (center) NBHOFL; (bottom left) NBHOFL; (right) UPI/Corbis; 45 (top) NBHOFL; (bottom) UPI/Corbis; 46 (top) Special Collections, California State University; (bottom, l-r) AP Photos; Mark Thiessen, NGS; Ken Viale; (baseball cards) NBHOFM; 47 (l-r) Milo Stewart Jr./NBHOFM; NBHOFL; NBHOFL; NBHOFL; 48 Les Stone

One of the world's largest nonprofit scientific and educational organizations, the National Geographic Society was founded in 1888 "for the increase and diffusion of geographic knowledge." Fulfilling this mission, the Society educates and inspires millions every day through its magazines, books, television programs, videos, maps and atlases, research grants, the National Geographic Bee, teacher workshops, and innovative classroom materials. The Society is supported through membership dues, charitable gifts, and income from the sale of its educational products. This support is vital to National Geographic's mission to increase global understanding and promote conservation of our planet through exploration, research, and education.

NATIONAL GEOGRAPHIC SOCIETY
1145 17th Street N.W. ◆ Washington, D.C. 20036-4688 ◆ U.S.A.
Visit the Society's Web site: www.nationalgeographic.com